AGING

TROUBLED

SOCIETY

AGING

Jonathan Bliss

The Rourke Corporation, Inc.
Vero Beach, Florida 32964

The Rourke Corporation, Inc.
P.O. Box 3328, Vero Beach, FL 32964

Bliss, Jonathan.
    Aging / by Bliss, Jonathan.
        p. cm. — (Troubled society)
    Includes bibliographical references and index.
    Summary: Takes a closer look at some of the myths of aging and discusses the ways that society deals with the aged in economic, political, social, and medical settings.
    ISBN 0-86593-114-3
    1. Aged—United States—Social conditions—Juvenile literature. 2. Aging—Social aspects—United States—Juvenile literature. [1. Old age.] I. Title. II. Series.
HQ1064.U5B45   1991
305.26'0973—dc20   91-10262
                                                                        CIP
                                                                        AC

Series Editor: Gregory Lee
Editors: Elizabeth Sirimarco, Marguerite Aronowitz
Book design and production: The Creative Spark,
    Capistrano Beach, CA
Cover photograph: Mike Douglas/The Image Works

Contents

ONE

THE CRISIS OF AGING

Most of us don't like to think about getting old. To the young, getting old means wrinkles and illness. The body and mind slow down. Growing old means growing useless. This is the way we often think about old people today—even our own grandparents. Most older folks seem kind and gentle, but for the most part, we don't really think of them as being good for much. They can't, for instance, throw a football 50 yards, or race around the block, or party all night.

Like most young people, you may think that when a person gets to be 65 or 70, it's pretty much time to check out. People retire, start gardening, maybe do a little traveling, then die quickly and without too much fuss. When we think of old people, we think of nursing homes, wheelchairs, senility, lingering illnesses, hospitals, and funerals.

Old age is nothing we really want to see or take part in. And since there are plenty of places to put our old folks, you usually don't have to. After all, the government has the situation under control, right? We're a rich country. We provide tons of services for our aging citizens: from free medical care to comprehensive social services. We have the best health care in the world. And if older people are down on their luck—we like to call it "being disadvantaged"—there's enough food, shelter, and help to go around. In addition, there are lots of homes where they can go to be with people their own age and keep out of the way. In fact, there is absolutely nothing we have to be concerned about.

Sounds good, pretty much like what you may

Sarah Saklad, 97, is congratulated by her son after receiving her high school diploma. Saklad and six other nursing home residents took courses for two years at Lowell High School in Massachusetts in order to graduate.

have been told—only none of it is true.

The stories and myths we've created about aging are untrue or out-of-date. The assumptions many people make about how well we take care of our aging population are wrong. The situation is definitely not under control. Medical care is not always available, and when it is, it's often inadequate. In fact, many old people in this country go hungry, don't get proper medical care, and haven't a place to stay. Money is not always available to help the elderly. And over the next 25 years, the situation may get much worse. In fact, the elderly will outnumber your own age group.

The purpose of this book is to discuss the myths about aging. You'll learn what is true and what isn't. We'll talk about the problems we face today in dealing with an aging population, the greater problems we will be encountering tomorrow, and the exciting ideas some people are coming up with to help solve these dilemmas.

Family Care

Today in America we have government programs that help the elderly. *Social Security* is a retirement plan that all working people contribute to. When they retire, they receive monthly payments from the Social Security fund. *Medicare* is a health program that helps retired people pay medical bills.

These programs are recent ideas. Before Social Security and Medicare, before retirement homes, before senior citizens had anything to fall back on, there was the family. The family was expected to take care of its own, from the youngest to the oldest. It was just part of the way things were.

Let's go back a few hundred years. If you were a member of a farming family—and back then most people were farmers—everyone in your family worked. Everyone helped till the soil, plant the seed, tend the animals, and harvest the crop. If you were a craftsman or merchant, your family supported the craft, and lived in the same house or town. Most of your needs were supplied by the family or community in which you lived. When you got old, you were looked after and respected. Rather than being considered useless, you were looked up to. It makes sense that with age comes wisdom. To suggest two or three hundred years ago that senior citizens should be sent to old-age homes would have been a crazy idea.

Many things were different in the old days. For example, in 14th century England, the average life expectancy of a man was about 25 years. People were often married at age 15 or 16 and considered middle-aged by the time they reached 21! And things hadn't changed much by the time of the American Revolution. In 1770, a child born in America could expect to live to age 35, and the average age of the population was around 16. One hundred years later, a person could count on living until he or she was 40, and the average age was 21. In other words, for most of the history of the United States, human population consisted largely of teenagers with a sprinkling of "old men and women" who lived beyond the normal age of 35. Of course, there were still people who managed to live into their seventies. Even the Bible talks about the normal life span of a man being "four score and ten," or 70 years. But the number of people who actually reached that age was tiny—less than five in every 100 people.

Why was it so difficult to grow old? First of all, it was hard to stay alive. Many children didn't survive infancy. Those who did faced fatal diseases, accidents, and wars. Measles, small pox, cholera, pneumonia, influenza, malnutrition, war—there were a million ways to die. In the 14th century, for example, the bubonic plague killed 20 million Europeans—one in every three persons. And as late as 1919, an influenza epidemic claimed 20 million people worldwide. As a result, very few people could expect to reach an advanced age.

You couldn't have an old-age problem when the average person lived to be only 40. Divorce was less of a problem too, since the average couple didn't live more than 18 months after their last child had left home. Understandably, America had little concern about their elderly population 100 years ago since there weren't many of them around. The few who survived were taken care of by their families.

Back in 1850, if your parents or grandparents were too old to work, you didn't ship them off to a nursing home, you cared for them at home. Occasionally the doctor might stop in if they were ill, but otherwise they were your responsibility. When they died, it was usually in their own bed, while the family stood by.

Was this a better attitude than the one we have today? In many respects it was. Children grew up with a sense of their roots, and grandparents saw

Thousands of elderly men and women live alone in single-room hotels such as this one in San Francisco. Senior Outreach programs are appearing in many cities to try and bring these people out of their isolation.

more of their grandchildren. Members of a family could get to know each other better than they do today. Members of the family found a greater sense of security and belonging than most of us have today. Natural processes like birth and death were less terrifying; death wasn't something you could ignore if you saw it happening in front of you. And dying was less lonely and frightening for the person who was passing away.

This old-fashioned family support system is still practiced by many cultures throughout the world. Even in America, many ethnic groups who live in large or "extended" families observe long valued traditions. In most Chinese families, for example, aging parents are taken in by the eldest son and his family. In Chinese culture the old are to be protected, respected, and obeyed. Even in modern-day Los Angeles, it is estimated that 70 percent of all the Chinese-American elderly live with and rely upon their families for support.

Tribes in Africa, Polynesia, and South America still function in family groups as they have for thousands of years. As a person ages in one of these societies, he or she becomes more respected. In fact, the leaders of most tribes are elder citizens. These are the people who make major decisions for the rest.

Change

Why did this way of caring for our elderly stop if it was so successful? A simple answer is that times change. And, as in most other areas of life, there was one major factor that made change inevitable: technology.

Advancing technology has made it more difficult for the family to stay together. For example, with the invention of cars, trains, and airplanes, it became easier to get around, to move away from family and friends. That meant that your uncle could leave the farm for a better job, or your sister could meet and marry someone from New York whom you never met. You could attend a college in some far away state and end up settling down in an area other than that of your parents and relatives.

Technology also meant industry, and people coming together in ever-expanding cities. With the growth of industry, people suddenly had more career choices. You didn't have to be a farmer like your parents if you didn't want to. You could move to the city, become a factory worker or a clerk, and perhaps earn three or four times as much as your parents did back on the farm.

Another important factor has been the advancement of medicine. If you were unlucky enough to get sick in 1450, it was almost impossible to see a doctor, since most towns and villages didn't have one. If you did, the doctor usually gave you a potion to swallow, or bled you to rid your body of vile spirits. And he probably wrapped you in bandages that were soaked in terrible-smelling liquids. If you were really unlucky, he might do surgery on you, using dirty knives and no painkillers. Nobody knew about germs in those days. If infection set in, the surgery was usually fatal. Most doctors killed more patients than they cured. A person was better off letting the body heal itself if it could.

Poor diets and unhealthy living conditions also used to kill a lot of people. In Europe before this century, one's diet consisted largely of meal or bread, a little meat or poultry and some ale. That was it. No vegetables to speak of, no dairy products, no fruit. It was hardly a balanced diet. Bathing was something you did once or twice a year. Because people lived in unhealthy conditions, drank polluted water and ate bad food, there was a far greater risk of getting sick than there is today.

Eventually, people learned about hygiene, cleanliness and sanitation. Frequent baths, airing their houses, and indoor plumbing improved health conditions. Doctors and scientists developed medicines to fight diseases like small pox and diphtheria that once killed millions. Antiseptic practices made childbirth and surgery safer. Penicillin was discovered. And preventive care protected many people against the diseases that were still left.

As more treatments and cures were made available and medical care got better, more children survived, fewer people died prematurely, and people started living longer. The world's population literally exploded in the 20th century. Within 30 years, the world's population had doubled. Fifteen years later, it had doubled again. Seven years later, it had doubled yet again. In 1900 the normal life expectancy of an American male was up to age 50; by 1985 that figure had climbed to 71 and was still rising. Women, who had always lived longer than men on average, went from a life expectancy of 55 to 78. As the longevity of Americans increased, so too did the number of people over age 65. In 1900, only four percent of the U.S. population was over 65; by 1980 this figure had jumped to 11 percent.

Once children could expect their parents to die before they became a burden. As parents began living into their 70s, 80s, and even 90s, however, they no longer fit into most children's plans. Families who lived together even after the children were grown usually did so out of financial need. Aging parents and grandparents often didn't want to become part of their children's modern lifestyle. In 1957, for example, only 26 percent of people 60 or older felt it was right to live with their grown children. Similar surveys conducted in 1976 and 1978

The Facts:
Aging In The United States

• Throughout most of recorded human history, only one in ten people could expect to live to age 65. Today, nearly 80 percent of Americans will live to be 65 or older.

• In July 1983, the number of Americans over the age of 65 surpassed the number of teenagers. We are no longer a nation of young people.

• With continuing improvements in lifestyle and medical technology, the over-65 population in the year 2000 is likely to be close to 45 million, representing as much as one-fifth of the total population.

• Of the 30 million Americans over 65, only 10 percent show any significant loss of memory, and fewer than half of those show any serious mental impairment.

• If the American Association of Retired Persons were to become an independent nation, its population would be slightly smaller than that of Argentina.

• In the most recent federal budget, subsidies for housing, meals, medical care, pensions, Social Security and other benefits for the elderly came to nearly 28 percent of the federal budget, equal to the amount spent on defense.

The late Claude Pepper of Florida was still going strong as a congressman at age 88.

found the elderly even less willing to live with their children.

Modern society seemed unable to cope with the life-extending miracles it had created, and the extended family—once its foundation—began to crumble. Confronted with a growing number of old people, government ignored the problem for as long as it could. This was easy to do. After all, older people had little influence on the country or industry that supported it. But this was about to change.

TWO

THE SAFETY NET

Cut loose from their families and ignored by the government, many elderly in this century were left without money, food, shelter, or medical care. This meant that as soon as a man retired, or a wife lost her husband, they were suddenly in a kind of financial free-fall, without any "safety net" to catch and protect them. The government wasn't about to do anything. Before 1935, almost no money in federal or state budgets was set aside for the elderly. This was an intolerable situation, and eventually politicians began to see it too.

The first step toward creating a safety net for this new aging population was taken by President Franklin Roosevelt in 1935, when he proposed and won approval for Social Security. This revolutionary new program set up a fund into which Americans paid some of their income during their working years. Once workers retired at age 65, the fund supplied them with a monthly income. As recently as 1951, the legal maximum contribution to the fund was $30 per year; today each person pays almost eight percent of his or her income earned under $32,500, or about $5,000.

Today Social Security is the major source of income for people over age 65. More than 90 percent of older persons are eligible for this program (about 37 million people as of 1990). The basic requirement for receiving Social Security is that the recipient must have worked at least ten years in some business or profession (or be a surviving spouse). Workers covered by Social Security pay a

These seniors don't seem to be taking their 62-year-old instructor very seriously during this exercise class in St. Louis.

tax on their earnings and employers pay an identical amount. This means that by the time a worker gets to be 65, he or she has usually contributed a large sum to the Social Security fund. The size of a worker's benefits reflects the level of earnings during the wage earner's working years. However, the fund guarantees a minimum monthly income of around $300 for an individual or $400 for an eligible couple, plus an annual cost-of-living increase.

Social Security has proven to be a hugely successful safety net. It not only provided a safety net for the elderly, but it also eased the worries of the growing middle-class population. For the first time,

Americans knew that when they retired there would be some financial assistance for them to draw on.

Social Security was a good beginning, but many people in this country realized it wasn't enough. Americans who had lived through the Great Depression of the 1930s wanted more security than they could get from just one program, like health care, for example.

Private industry tried to fill some of the gaps with the introduction of better pension and retirement programs. But this was not enough. Social Security did not provide the money to pay for increasing medical bills. If something truly catastrophic happened—like a long hospital stay or major surgery—for most people there was no way to pay the bills. Finally, in 1965, the Medicare and Medicaid programs were created. The government also established the Administration on Aging. This body would oversee the distribution of federal money to people over 60. Under Medicare and Medicaid, any senior citizen was assured of receiving proper medical care, no matter how much it cost.

Other programs soon followed, such as the Age Discrimination Bill (1967); the Supplemental Security Program (1972) which guarantees all older Americans a minimum income; and Catastrophic Health Insurance (1988). All these bills and new programs meant more money and more rights for the elderly. They also meant more money spent by federal, state, and local governments. Huge bureaucracies were created to control the distribution of funds.

By the 1980s, many government officials felt

The Facts:
Aging In The United States

• If the Social Security system is not changed, it will soon take two people their entire working lives to pay for the Social Security benefits of one retired person.

• The first baby boomers will hit traditional retirement age around 2011. Within 15 years after that, Social Security will begin running huge annual deficits without new sources of funding.

• While the average income earned by the head of the household over 65 is the lowest of any age group ($19,816), their discretionary income (that money they have to spend on leisure) is the highest ($5,633).

• One-third of the $450 billion spent annually on health care goes to the 12 percent of the population over 65.

• More than 50,000 people participated in regional "Senior Olympics" in 50 cities across the country in 1987.

• Over the next decade, the retirement housing market, now worth $3 billion per year, is expected to rise to more than $35 billion per year.

they had solved one of the country's greatest problems. America's old people would be well cared for, or so it was believed. Social Security, Medicare and Medicaid promised to supplement private pension and retirement plans. Many things supported this optimism. The over-65 crowd now had more money to spend on nonessential things like travel and leisure, and they enjoyed more benefits than any other age group in this country. These were good times for retirees, and working people talked fondly of what they would do once they retired. If there were going to be problems down the road, few people wanted to think about it.

Holes in the Safety Net

America's vast safety net had not been erected without problems or without considerable cost to the taxpayer. Money for housing, medical care, pensions, Social Security and other benefits for the elderly came to nearly 28 percent of the federal budget—equal to the amount spent on defense.

Fifteen years earlier, in 1965, this commitment had seemed pretty impressive. Social Security and other programs for people over 65 appeared successful. But by 1980 there was trouble on the horizon. Three reasons became cause for worry: the increased life expectancy, decreased number of births, and aging of the *baby boomers* (people born between 1946 and 1964).

The most sobering change in the recent population was the aging of the baby boomers. This group has always been huge: more than one-third of all Americans, or 76 million people. In 1890, there were only 2.4 million Americans over 65, or less than four percent of the nation's population. By the end of this century there will be 35 million Americans of that age, or 13 percent of the total population. The number of Americans over 65 has already surpassed the number of teenagers.

Population Shifts

In addition to increased numbers of people, we are also living longer: 28 years have been added to a person's average life expectancy since 1900. A child born in 1989 can now expect to reach age 75. By the year 2040, the National Institute on Aging predicts that most men will live to age 86 and most women will make it to 91.5 years of age. This means that in only 200 years, the average American's life expectancy will have doubled. Not only are people living longer, they're staying healthier for a longer time.

This is good news for those who will be able to enjoy those extra retirement years, but it's not such good news for those who must pay for it. While the number of seniors is exploding upward, the number of children who will earn money to support Social Security is going down. And people aren't having as many babies as they used to. The rate of childbirth in America is down to 1.8 children per couple, which is 27 percent lower than the rate in 1970. This means that Americans aren't even reproducing enough to replace themselves. While this is probably a good thing for the earth's resources, it is poor timing for those of us who plan to retire in the next 25 years.

By the year 2040, the National Institute on

Studies show that people who remain active and interested in their work and hobbies tend to stay healthier and live longer.

Aging projects that 87 million Americans will be over age 65. While our great-grandparents felt lucky to see age 50 or 60, most Americans today can hope to be healthy and active at age 80, 90, and even 100. Even our definition of "old age" will change. Because more people over 65 now remain vigorous and healthy, many of them must be classified as middle-aged instead of elderly. In the coming years the term "elderly" may not be an appropriate term to use for someone less than 85 or 90 years old.

When the baby boomers reach 65 and show no signs of dying, or even slowing down, who will pay to support them? What happens when they start asking for Social Security and pension benefits they worked so hard to earn? How will the younger generation, already outnumbered by their elders, come up with the money to keep the system afloat? Unless things change considerably, there is no way Social Security or any of the other federally-funded programs will survive.

If we don't solve these problems, we will have a national disaster on our hands: too many retired people and not enough money. What are we going to do?

THREE

AGING AND POLITICS

Many elderly people have influenced American politics. Many of the wealthiest individuals in our society have lived the longest, and wealth has a way of affecting both politicians and policy. There are also quite a few politicians—especially those in Congress—who continue to serve well into their 70s and 80s. These senior citizens certainly possess political power. But the rise of the elderly as a powerful political *lobby*—a group working to influence public policy—is a recent event.

Before 1950 the elderly had practically no political presence. Only one government program concerned the elderly: Social Security. The fact that such a measure existed at all was due less to pressure from the elderly than the efforts of President Franklin Roosevelt.

Social Security was a product of the stock market crash of 1929 and the Great Depression that followed it. The 1930s were the most miserable economic times anyone had ever seen. In America 20 percent of the population was unemployed. People were starving and homeless, and banks and businesses went broke every day. During this bleak period, Roosevelt made the country two promises: first, he would see that things got better, and second, he would make sure that it never happened again. Social Security was one of the things he did to make good on his second promise.

It took another 25 years and a population of several million more Americans over 65 before

These students are part of SeniorNet, a program based at the University of San Francisco that teaches computer skills to people 55 and older.

senior citizens finally found their political voice. It also took organizing.

The first rumbles from this growing constituency (voting bloc) came from Florida. By 1960, Florida had the largest concentration of retired people in the country. In such numbers, it was easier for seniors to focus on their problems. Issues such as inadequate funding for medical care, more public housing for the elderly, and more benefits than Social Security alone could provide. Times were getting tougher.

The cost of living kept going up while the income of most retirees remained fixed. Most senior citizens could no longer live comfortably on what Social Security was providing.

Surviving financially, however, was not their only concern. To most older Americans, the main complaint was the way society viewed them. The attitude seemed to be that senior citizens were washed up, useless, and a burden on society. Many seniors felt this was ridiculous, like discrimination. Since Americans were living longer, they were also living healthier, and it wasn't unusual to see a man or woman in their 70s acting and working like someone in their 30s or 40s. So why were they being forced to retire at age 65? Why were they being shuttled off to old-age homes and retirement communities when they still wanted to live in their own homes and help their neighbors? Older Americans didn't want to be pushed aside when they felt they still had a lot to offer.

Seniors wanted an end to age discrimination. But who was going to speak for them? Who was going to champion their cause? There was no one in Washington to represent them, and no one in the country was offering to be their voice.

In 1962, they found a voice: Senator Claude Pepper. He sponsored a bill that had created the National Cancer Institute and the National Institute of Health—two of the most worthwhile organizations Washington had ever created. Pepper was also involved in the creation of the World Health Organization and was a sponsor of the nation's first minimum wage bill.

After his long term in the Senate Pepper lost his bid for renomination in 1950 and retired to practice law. By 1962, however, times were changing. At age 62, Pepper ran for the House of Representatives and was elected, becoming one of the oldest "freshman" congressmen in American history. In the years that followed, he became a champion for the rights of senior citizens. He became Chairman of the House Select Committee on Aging, and later the Chairman of the powerful Rules Committee.

His continuing influence in Washington was a result of the growing number of older people, and his own vitality. At 88, when most people are supposed to be retired, Congressman Claude Pepper was still a man to whom millions of senior citizens turned when they had a problem. He wore trifocals, twin hearing-aids, a pacemaker, and an artificial heart valve, but no one could tell Pepper he wasn't doing his job. A colorful orator, he made speeches and affected public policy right up until the moment of his death at age 89.

While Pepper was working in Washington, activist Maggie Kuhn was working just as hard in New York and San Francisco. In 1970, at the age of 65, she had been forced to retire from her job. She took this as an insult both to her personally and to her age group in general. She and five of her friends who had also lost their jobs "for being too old" decided to band together and form a radical group committed to fighting "ageism." As part of their tactics, they held public demonstrations and sit-ins to make themselves visible. They called themselves the "Consultation of Older and Younger Adults," but a TV

The late Claude Pepper chaired the House Select Committee on Aging, where he
was a respected watchdog for the elderly in Congress. Here he meets Maggie
Kuhn of the Gray Panthers, a group that advocates the rights of the elderly.

newsman dubbed them "Gray Panthers." The name stuck.

For nearly two decades, Maggie Kuhn has continued her crusade against America's outdated attitude regarding the elderly. Vital and fiercely intelligent, she has created an organization that today has more than 74,000 members and chapters in 30 states. Her mission remains the same: to change America's treatment of the elderly.

Under the leadership of people like Kuhn and Pepper, the senior movement gained momentum, and organizations were formed to advance the cause of America's senior citizens. During the past 25 years, senior support and advocacy groups have grown at an astonishing pace. Today, for example, there are:

- 20,000 seniors in the Older Women's League (OWL)
- 74,000 in the activist Gray Panthers
- 2.2 million members in the conservative National Alliance of Senior Citizens (NASC)
- 4.5 million in the 4,000 local chapters of the National Council of Senior Citizens (NCSC)
- 30 million members in the American Association of Retired Persons (AARP), second only to the American Automobile Association in size

Of all these organizations, the AARP is surely the most influential. Founded in 1958, it now commands the attention of many lawmakers. Its legislative staff in Washington numbers 125, and there are 20 full-time lobbyists.

The growth of the senior movement, from Claude Pepper to the Gray Panthers to the AARP, is remarkable. These days, what the "gray lobby"

Dan Lago founded People and Animals Coming Together (PACT) so that many elderly could share their need for companionship with a cat or dog. Lago provides animals to both seniors living alone and in nursing homes.

wants, it usually gets. Over the last 25 years Congress has overseen the enactment of many important bills to improve the quality of life for the elderly, including the following:

- Medicare and Medicaid bills (1965)
- Older Americans Act which established the Administration for Aging (1965)
- Age Discrimination in Employment Act (1967)
- Supplemental Social Security Program guaranteeing all older Americans a minimum income (1972)
- Social Security indexing to inflation (1972)

- Establishment of Federal Council for Aging (1973)
- Social Security reform (1983)
- Age of mandatory retirement eliminated (1986)
- Catastrophic health insurance established (1988)

As an example of just how powerful this lobby has become, the Older Americans Act was first funded in 1965 at $5 million. In 1988, it received over $1 billion of the federal budget! At the same time, Medicare has grown from a $35 million program in 1980 to a $91 million program in 1988. According to one research organization in Washington, D.C., by the year 2000 more than 32 percent of the federal budget will be spent on programs for the elderly.

Not all is bright and wonderful for the elderly. In 1990, Congress did an abrupt about-face, repealing the Catastrophic Health Insurance Act of 1988. This marked a major defeat for the senior citizen lobby and indicated an unwillingness on the part of a conservative president and his administration to support an increase in health care for the elderly. Does this reversal indicate a permanent step backward for senior citizens? One thing is certain: the federal funds currently earmarked for the elderly are insufficient for the job ahead. Aging baby boomers will soon overwhelm the system if no more is done. Luckily, there are solutions that may help avoid a catastrophe, as you will see in the next chapters.

FOUR

AGING AND EMPLOYMENT

Many people still believe that getting old means getting feeble. We tend to assume that a man or woman in their 60s is "past their prime" or "over the hill." One of the basic assumptions of our society seems to be that a 70-year-old man or woman cannot work or think as well as a man or woman in their 30s. This, of course, is not true, and history bears this out.

Michelangelo was appointed architect of St. Peter's Cathedral in Rome at age 71. Pablo Casals, the world-famous cellist, was performing concerts at age 88. Grandma Moses didn't even start to paint until she was in her 80s. Jonas Salk, the creator of the polio vaccine, is doing important AIDS research at age 73. Armand Hammer, founder of Occidental Petroleum (one of the largest corporations in America) worked a 14-hour day right up to the time of his death at age 88. Sam Walton, owner of Wal-Mart Stores and one of the country's wealthiest men, is still working a full day at age 80. Oscar-winning actress Jessica Tandy and her actor-husband Hume Cronyn are both 80-plus. President Ronald Reagan finished his second term at the age of 77.

If you look at the people who run America's major corporations, most of them are over 60. In fact, of the 900 largest corporations in the United States, the average age of board members is 62.

And it's not just the rich and famous who continue to work. Many people are discovering that traditional retirement doesn't appeal to them. In a recent poll, the majority of seniors asked said they

Karl Augustin of France may be the oldest newspaper editor in the world: he's more than 100 years old.

would continue to work in one way or another after 65—even if they had enough money to live comfortably. The reason? They like working.

Americans come from a tradition of hard work; we find it difficult to respect people who don't work. The work ethic of earlier generations is in our blood, and the idea of an honest day's pay for an honest day's work is strongly felt by most people. We have been taught that work is an obligation, a necessity of life. Even when we "play," most of us are really working. For example, we *practice* football or basketball, we *work* at improving our swimming or skiing, and we *study* crossword puzzles or chess. Little wonder that many are unprepared for the lifestyle of retirement and prefer the stress of work.

Another reason for staying on the job is that in our fast-moving, impersonal society, work is sometimes the best place people can go to socialize. Our jobs have traditionally been a place for making friends and receiving approval.

Given the number of hours most people work in today's society, they are likely to spend more time at the office than at home. In fact, we often spend more time with our co-workers than with our spouses and children. In a recent poll, when asked whether they would rather work at home or in a central office, most people responded that they preferred working in an office. For many people, it is the closest thing they have to a family.

It's no wonder then that for many people, retiring from a responsible, full-time job is hard. Instead of being surrounded by people who depend on them, they stay in an apartment or home that has a TV and maybe a pet for company. How many times have you heard about someone dying only a few months or years after retiring? In many cases, the stress of doing nothing, or feeling like an outcast, is too much for them.

So why not continue to work into your 70s and 80s? Is this easy to do? While 60 percent of all senior citizens still choose to retire in their later years, a growing number now opt for at least a part-time job. There are several factors which make work more attractive than it used to be. For example, people who are challenged by their work are more likely to continue working long after the normal age for retirement. Judges, politicians, physicians, college professors, musicians and composers, writers, reporters, and entrepreneurs work long past retirement age. More than three times as many doctors as other health-service people keep working past age 65. Lawyers are seven times more likely to continue working than laborers, and college professors are four times as likely as garbage collectors to stay in their jobs past retirement age.

Before 1978, most people had no choice about retiring. When a person reached 65, the boss held a party for them, a gold watch was pushed into their hands, and they were launched into their "golden years"—whether they wanted to be or not. Retirement was strictly enforced and, said many people, necessary to make room for younger workers.

By the 1980s, this approach had lost its appeal. For one thing, new workers didn't always perform as good a job as the seniors they replaced. In a few more years, there wouldn't be enough young people to replace the older people in any case. In the so-called "service industries," restaurants and retail stores were suddenly having trouble replacing their older waiters, waitresses, and salespeople.

Many seniors wanted to keep on working if they could. Washington finally heard them, and in 1976 pushed back the mandatory age of retirement to 70. Twelve years later, the mandatory age of retirement was eliminated altogether.

Seniors now had the opportunity to work as long as they were able, but it did not always follow that businesses wanted to give them this chance. Certain prejudices run deep in any human society, and no prejudice is more acceptable to a lot of people than ageism—the belief that an older worker is less effective than the younger worker. This bias has its roots in the conventional image of an old man: doddering, forgetful, sluggish. Business has traditionally cleared away older employees on practical grounds: older employees are more likely to get sick, become permanently disabled, or die. And few businesses want to pay the steep fees that health insurance companies demand to cover such employees.

But time has changed much of this. Owing to better nutrition, better health care, and more exercise, an older worker is now less likely to become unfit to work. At the same time, the nature of work has changed as well. Most jobs no longer require strength over brains. In our "post-industrial" age, more and more jobs are based on knowledge, experience and judgment—not muscles. The tools of this new age are not picks and shovels but computers and telephones. The rules of the game have simply changed.

In an age when many potential workers well over 65 remain alert and vital, it seems shortsighted to punish them for outdated attitudes. The argument against hiring older workers for health reasons no longer makes sense. The government (through Medicare and Medicaid) covers most senior citizens without additional contributions from the employer. In an era when younger employees can be illiterate, unmotivated or scarce, employers are becoming more and more aware of this experienced and willing resource called the senior citizen.

Put simply, American business will have to

take advantage of this new work force if they want to survive. The AARP, citing U.S. census figures, projects that there will be five million fewer people between the ages of 18 and 24 entering the job market in 1995 than there are today. At the same time, according to the U.S. Department of Labor, the economy is expected to generate 16 million new jobs. Three of every four of these new jobs will require education beyond high school. Only one segment of society can supply the army of employees needed to help America overcome this job crisis: the ranks of senior citizens. By 1995, some 35 million elderly Americans will be available—if industry wants to hire them.

Many employers are already taking advantage of this resource. Wherever you go, you'll see older Americans holding down jobs traditionally done by teenagers and young adults. McDonald's, Burger King, and many other fast-food chains now have aggressive policies to hire senior citizens. Many department stores, such as Macy's and Bloomingdale's, desperate for experienced help, are hiring older applicants because they find them more reliable and responsible. And they don't usually demand high salaries. Universities often encourage professors to remain on faculty beyond their normal retirement age. And many corporations retain their older managers by hiring them back as consultants after they retire.

As more jobs become available to them, and the need to supplement their shrinking incomes becomes more pressing, senior citizens are returning to the job market in ever-increasing numbers. To

Another Look At Aging

• The secret to staying young is to live honestly, eat slowly, and lie about your age.
> —*Lucille Ball*

• Old age is not for sissies.
> —*Variously ascribed*

• Old age is like a plane flying through the storm. Once you are aboard there is nothing you can do.
> —*Golda Meir*

• When I was young there was no respect for the young, and now that I am old there is no respect for the old. I missed out coming and going.
> —*J.B. Priestley*

• You know you're old when you notice how young the derelicts are getting.
> —*Jeanne Phillips*

• I smoke cigars because at my age if I don't have something to hold onto I might fall down.
> —*George Burns*

• If I had known I was going to live this long I would have taken better care of myself.
> —*Leon Eldred*

• I don't worry about getting old. I'm old already. Only young people worry about getting old.
> —*George Burns*

• To me, old age is fifteen years older than I am.
> —*Bernard M. Baruch*

handle this older work force, companies are changing work styles. For example, more part-time and flex-time jobs (with flexible work hours) are becoming available, giving older workers their choice of days and hours. Businesses are also learning that older employees can be given new skills with retraining. Many re-education centers across the country report that older students are more willing to work and are more attentive in class. They also tend to score higher on tests than many of their younger, less motivated classmates. One federally funded program, the Service Corps of Retired Executives (SCORE), recruits retired businessmen to help small businesses get stated. This program has proven to be very successful and shows that retired executives can continue contributing to society and business long after their official retirement.

There is a new focus on what the word "employee" really means. Today's employee can often do much of what he or she does at work in the home. By using computers, fax machines and modems, the "home office" allows many retired people to return to work without leaving home. Older workers are also creating their own small businesses. Self-employed business people, after all, are unlikely to discriminate against others like themselves on the basis of age.

An alternative to retirement is offered by Japan. Retirement there differs fundamentally from the United States. In Japan, people work as long as they are able, so the country avoids the burden of able but unproductive citizens. Instead, Japanese workers usually "retire" from their jobs before age 60,

Many people over age 65 still enjoy working, like this crossing guard.

but don't quit working. They lose their seniority, normal salary, and usual authority, but not the chance to work. In retiring from their main jobs so early, they can re-educate and move into another field if they want to.

Whether we use the Japanese example or create our own way of handling retirement, there is little doubt that the employee of tomorrow will be significantly different from the employee of today. Ageism and other forms of discrimination may still exist in the future, but business is unlikely to pass up a good thing. If it is profitable to hire senior citizens, then businesses will gladly accept this willing group of workers and embrace the new era.

FIVE

AGING AND MEDICAL CARE

Although people may live longer now and are healthier for more years, eventually the statistics catch up with all of us. For example, 22 percent of all Americans over 65 are disabled.

Eventually, the body wears out. We move slower, think slower, and get tired more easily. We can fall prey to one of the many diseases that medicine still can't cure, like cancer, senility, arthritis, osteoporosis, and Parkinsonism. When that happens, people need care and caregivers: doctors, nurses, hospitals, and especially family members. If you can't afford these things, if you aren't getting the care you need, then the system isn't working for you.

Right now, the system is working for most people —barely. But with the fastest-growing segment of the U.S. population being the 85-and-older age group, and the baby boomers coming up fast on their retirement years, the problems are sure to get bigger.

One of the biggest problems Americans face right now is the high cost of medical care. Science has provided many new tools and drugs for detecting and curing disease. Many deadly illnesses are now curable; many more can be treated before they become killers. However, many medical procedures are very expensive.

In many countries around the world free medical care is available to all citizens, no matter what the cost or the illness. In the United States, however,

This man's wife suffers from Alzheimer's disease, a disease that has no cure yet. A person with Alzheimer's gradually loses the ability to recognize their loved ones, or take care of themselves.

the government has attempted to protect both the right of the health industry to remain profitable and the right of the individual to choose whatever medical care he or she desires. The result is that the price of medical care has gone through the roof. It is not uncommon for one surgical operation to cost more than $50,000; the cost of open-heart or transplant surgery can easily exceed $100,000. A 15-minute session under a CAT or MRI scanner (sophisticated detection devices) can run over $1,000. The cost of one anti-immune drug—necessary to help the body ward off attack after a transplant operation—can be more than $350 per week.

The sicker a person is, the more costly it becomes to keep them alive. Needless to say, most people don't have this kind of money. Even young people who are still working full-time may spend a lifetime paying back the medical establishment for just one procedure. What about older people who must undergo several procedures? How much can one person afford to pay for the care they receive?

Statistics show they can pay a great deal. In 1987, for example, Americans spent $443 billion on personal health care; by the year 2000 this country is expected to spend $1.4 trillion! That's more money than we spend for any other activity, including national defense, public and private education, or personal recreation. The cost of medical care is 20 times what it was 25 years ago, while the cost of everything else is only three times higher.

Why is it costing so much more for medicine than for food, gasoline, or housing? For one thing, it costs a lot of money to develop these marvelous inventions that keep us alive. It also costs a lot for the average hospital to care for a patient. The staff is usually large, the equipment is expensive and sophisticated, and the facilities must be constantly expanded and remodeled to meet increasing demands for service. Then there's the doctor, whose average annual salary has gone from about $15,000 in 1950 to around $65,000 in 1990. In addition to these expenses are the medical specialists such as the anesthesiologist or surgeon who usually make a salary above $100,000 a year.

Since almost no one is rich enough to cover

today's medical expenses by themselves, most Americans have medical insurance. Basically, this is a gambling proposition: the insurance company is betting that you won't get sick, while you are protecting yourself against the possibility that you will. If you do get sick, it is the medical insurer who pays most of your hospital and doctor bills, and the cost of prescription drugs. If you stay healthy, you still pay the insurer a regular annual sum (called a *premium*) which covers you for that year.

To stay profitable, insurers are usually only interested in covering you if they believe you won't get sick. As the possibility of illness increases with age, their willingness to insure you decreases. And under the current laws, it is perfectly legal for an insurance carrier to cancel your policy if your medical bills get too high. Either that, or they raise the premiums until you can no longer afford to keep the policy. It was for this reason that the federal government established Medicare and Medicaid, to help pay the medical bills of people who can't.

More recently, the government backed away from their role as insurer when in 1990 they repealed the Catastrophic Health Insurance Act. This will make it much harder for many senior citizens to pay the big bills, and adds to the already large problem faced by the elderly today.

The fees that doctors and hospitals want to charge for their services, however, do not always agree with what the government or insurance companies are willing to pay. This disagreement has caused the government and other insurers to set price limits on various types of medical procedures.

Under this arrangement, the insurer agrees to pay a fixed amount of money for an operation, treatment, or examination—and not one penny more. Naturally, this has been challenged by the medical establishment, which argues that their costs for doing business are rising even faster than the prices they charge for medical care.

Such a complex issue takes time and thought to solve, and many Americans will suffer if this isn't solved soon. Many emergency rooms and hospitals across the country have already been forced to close their doors because there wasn't enough money coming in to keep them profitable.

Another problem area is malpractice insurance. A small but increasing number of doctors are either leaving the profession or choosing to go into less specialized areas in order to avoid the steep cost of their own insurance. Malpractice insurance protects them in case they are sued.

Several alternatives to traditional medical care have also been tried to keep the cost of health care reasonable. The most successful of these is called the *health maintenance organization (HMOs)*. HMOs charge an annual fee per person, and in return provide complete medical coverage. While this program has proven to be a successful option to high-priced specialists and skyrocketing hospital costs, it limits the choice of which doctors you can see. Some people feel uncomfortable seeing a doctor they don't know, and there have been occasional debates about whether the quality of HMO medical care is as high as elsewhere.

Among the many plans being proposed

today, the most promising (and controversial) would be the creation of a National Health Insurance plan like those in countries such as Canada, England, France, and Sweden. A National Health Insurance program would cover all Americans, no matter what their illness, and no matter what the price. The government would pay for everything.

The advantages of such a system are obvious: never again would Americans have to worry about their health care. From cradle to grave their health care would be assured. The down side is that it would cost a lot of money: $150 billion a year or more, paid for by taxes. That would take a sizeable chunk out of everyone's salary. Doctors and many other health professionals are firmly against such a plan, but there are many government officials who support it. Many feel, however, that eventually some form of national health insurance will become law. This would mean that senior citizens of the future would have an even more comprehensive program of medical care than is currently available.

Nursing Homes

Health care often extends beyond the hospital or doctor's waiting room. For those elderly who require intensive nursing or *convalescent* care, America has seen the growth of "nursing homes." Many of these are excellent; however, in the last 20 years, stories of inadequate or negligent care have been in the news. In many instances, these places are merely storage areas where the elderly are kept sedated and confined without proper food, clothing, or sanitation. Federal, state, and local agencies

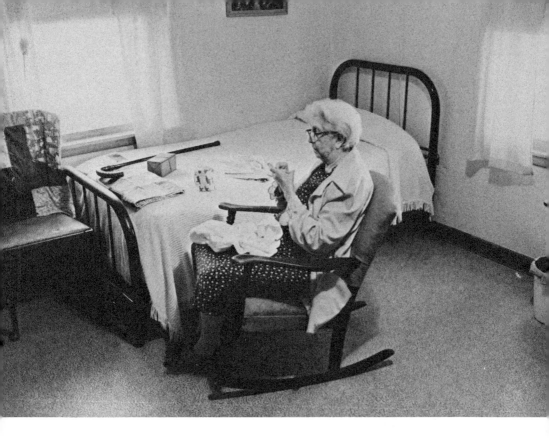

Nursing home life is a relatively new concept, and has separated many older people from their families and friends when they can no longer take care of themselves.

have been trying to crack down on these nursing homes, and keep better track of how they are being run. Thankfully, the nursing home scandal is beginning to fade. Homes that remain open have to be licensed and are generally clean and well-tended. Unfortunately, however, many are also too expensive for most people. It isn't uncommon for a good nursing home to charge $35,000 or more per year for their services—more than most families have.

Luckily, the financial burden of long-term care and the need for new nursing homes should be lightened by the growing trend toward home health care. In fact, federal spending for these health care options more than doubled between 1978 and 1984. One of these programs, Meals On Wheels, has become popular in many cities and states. Meals On Wheels provides hot, nutritious meals for those seniors who want to live alone but can no longer cook for themselves. This trend toward keeping the senior citizen independent and in his or her own home will continue to grow, and by the 2020s the baby boom is likely to have spawned a do-it-yourself home-health-care movement.

Still, in the future there will be enormous demand for affordable, long-term health care. The nation will have to find enough nurses and other service personnel to care for millions of aging baby boomers. The demand for nurses alone will easily outstrip society's capacity to provide them.

Millions of the future aged will depend heavily on government and private institutions to provide facilities and care. Just as schools and colleges had to be built and expanded in the 1950s and 1960s to accommodate the baby boomers when they were young, hundreds of new hospitals, nursing and retirement homes, and cemeteries must be built in the early part of the next century to accommodate them when they get old.

SIX

HOPEFUL SIGNS

While many problems having to do with aging remain to be solved, there are many reasons for optimism as well. One is found in the area of medicine. Many diseases that have been the most deadly are finally giving way to cures. For example, over the last 50 years the number one killer in the United States has been heart disease, accounting for half of all deaths. Yet recently, there have been dramatic changes in the lifestyles of young and middle-aged Americans. They are eating healthier foods, exercising more, and smoking less. This is beginning to decrease the rate of heart disease. Combined with medical advances, this change should bring a dramatic reduction in heart attacks, strokes, and related ailments in the years to come.

The same seems true for cancer, the number two killer of people over 65. Scientists are now working on the basic mechanisms that cause cancer, and researchers seem certain that within the next few decades, cures for many types of cancer will be found.

Similar optimism can be found among scientists researching such devastating diseases of the brain as Alzheimer's. New research could hold promise for increasing the quality of life for people with the disease. It seems likely that the future may bring a cure that will eliminate the disease altogether.

There have also been major advances made in correcting eyesight and hearing losses, reducing *osteoporosis* (a degeneration of the bone), curing *Parkinson's Disease* (a nervous disorder), and control-

As researchers learn more about the diseases that afflict the elderly, aging will be a less frightening process.

ling various kidney and urinary problems.

In fact, basic research is now being done on the nature of aging itself. Through genetic engineering, scientists are now studying human chromosomes and genes in search of the mechanisms that make us age. Could it be that there is a gene that determines when we get old? If there is, can it be modified? The subject touches our deepest hopes and fears. Is it possible that our life could be extended beyond 100 to 150 years, maybe even 200?

Recent research reports interesting findings. In a UCLA laboratory, Roy Walford, a professor of pathology, has been keeping mice on a strict diet that limits their intake to the very minimum. Not only does he get mice that are very lean, but they're also long-lived. His diet has effectively doubled, even tripled their normal life expectancy. In another experiment, Walford has succeeded in extending the life of several animals by reducing their body temperatures as little as three degrees. Like the *yogis* of India, who combine ultra-low-calorie diets with meditation, Walford believes that humans may be able to extend their lives through mind control and diet. Walford has become the chief "guinea pig" for his own experiments by living on a minimal diet and meditating every day.

Life extension has become such a popular topic that several books written on the subject have made the best-seller lists. In these books, various ways are proposed for extending life, from restricting eating to meditation to various vitamin regimens.

By the year 2020, many scientists fully expect people to be living into their 90s and 100s. The fastest growing segment of society will be over 100. Not only will there be more very old people around, but many of them will be vital, alert, and capable of doing the same work they did in their 30s or 40s. So the question for tomorrow remains the same as today: Will society take full advantage of this resource?

If we can judge by what's happening today, the answer should be yes. There are now numerous organizations devoted to the concerns of older people. AARP, the Gray Panthers, Americans for Generational Equity (AGE), the National Council of Senior Citizens (NSCS), the Older Women's League

(OWL)—these are but a few of a large number of organizations dedicated to the elderly. Many are powerful political forces, like the AARP, who can influence votes in Congress and push through legislation they see as vital to senior citizens.

Government agencies also contribute to financial aid and oversee problems associated with aging. For example, the federal government's Administration on Aging and the Federal Council on Aging help promote and pay for federal programs for the aging. Almost every state now has a Department of Aging that is responsible for overseeing the development of statewide programs for the elderly. In addition, there are numerous regional and local programs that help seniors cope with such problems as illness and housing, or offer recreational and educational opportunities.

Seniors are also being encouraged to take advantage of many educational programs offered throughout the U.S. More than 1,000 colleges and universities now encourage citizens over 65 to take classes for credit, and more than 120 schools have adopted special programs especially for older learners. In California's huge state college and university system, the average age of students has been going up steadily since the mid-'80s, in part due to an ever-increasing number of senior-citizen students.

City University of New York today counts more than 2,000 over-65 students, double the number enrolled in 1980. Harvard's Institute for Learning in Retirement has older Americans both as professors and students. Eckerd College's Academy of Senior Professionals in St. Petersburg, Florida, has more

Just a little batting practice in St. Petersburg, Florida. None of these baseball
enthusiasts is under 90 years old.

than 120 retirees as advisors and career counselors
to 1,200 young liberal arts students. Another interesting new trend in education is being pioneered by
Elderhostel, a self-supporting, nonprofit organization
based in Boston that has been combining leisure,
learning, and travel for older Americans since 1975.

Scientists who study aging or *gerontologists*
are discovering that elderly people who continue
educating themselves stay intellectually sharper
and are less likely to grow senile. The human brain,
it seems, benefits from exercise no less than human
muscles, and education is one of the best forms of
exercise the brain can get.

Speaking of muscles, it's long been assumed
that athletes are washed up by the time they hit age

40 or 50: their coordination and stamina goes, their legs and arms give out, and they're simply no match for their younger, quicker, stronger competitors. Not true. It seems that in the last few years more professional athletes are delaying their retirements and continuing successful careers. Take Nolan Ryan, the fire-balling right-handed pitcher who has established many records, including the all-time record for most strikeouts and most no-hit games. Now over 40, he has no plans for retirement. Ryan credits his incredible longevity in the game to modern training techniques and a healthy lifestyle.

Other athletes have similar stories: Joe Niekro was a starting pitcher until he was 43. Gordie Howe, one of the greatest hockey players of all time, was still playing at age 50. Sam Snead won a pro golf tournament when he was in his 70s, and George Foreman fought for the heavyweight championship of boxing at age 45.

Amateurs too have taken advantage of new attitudes and training techniques to do incredible things at an advanced age. Hulda Crooks, 91, has climbed 97 peaks since she was 65. Eighty-five-year-old Eric De Reynier took up hang-gliding at 72. Jane Stovall, 103, is a tango dancer, golf champion and student pilot at age 80. Sarah Conley, 104, recently graduated from De Anza College in Cupertino, California. Hundreds of senior citizens across the United States compete yearly in track and field events, like the Senior Olympics and the New York Marathon.

If senior citizens are discovering they can work and play like younger people, they are also realizing

The Facts:
Aging In The United States

• The divorce rate for people over 60 is now increasing as rapidly as that for younger age groups. Eighty percent of those who divorce remarry, and fully half of these second marriages also end in divorce.

• Of the total population of older Americans, 43 percent are single.

• The average American woman can expect to spend more years caring for her parents than she did caring for her children.

• The highest concentration of senior Americans can be found in two states: California and Florida.

• People who reach age 65 have a 44 percent chance of spending some time in a nursing home before they die.

• Currently, more than 1.5 million Americans live in nursing homes. More than 45 percent are age 85 or older, and more than 73 percent are female.

• Americans spent $40.6 billion on nursing home care in 1987.

they can enjoy themselves like never before. Recreation-oriented retirement communities are springing up all over the country.

Leisure World in Southern California has established dozens of mini-cities that cater to every need of the senior citizen. With golf courses, tennis, dancing, social and cultural clubs, elderly members often find themselves living more active and exciting lives than they did before their retirement. Sun City in Arizona is one of several cities expressly designed and developed for the growing senior population. In Sun City, every possible need is met, including the city's own college, bike and jogging tracks, and a concert hall.

Another new experiment in senior living is being provided by the "lifestyle town," which appeals to specific senior interests. One example, Worman's Hill near Frederick, Maryland, is modeled after an old-fashioned farming village where residents raise their own animals and sell home-made crafts to visitors in their own stores. Heritage Village, a 32-acre village near Grand Rapids, Michigan, focuses on the history and culture of Michigan and is staffed by 350 elder residents. Byron Park, a 186-unit development in Walnut Creek, California, has reproduced an 18th-century English country inn.

Many magazines are dedicated to senior citizens, including *Longevity, Senior World, Modern Maturity, Lear's, Second Wind*, and *Renaissance. Modern Maturity*, the first and most popular of the over-50 magazines, recently became the largest-circulation magazine in America, with 18 million subscribers and an estimated 30 million readers. By the

Aging in the United States of America today can be a warm, positive experience shared with family, or a lonely, isolated conclusion to one's life.

mid-1990s every major magazine publishing company will need a special publication geared to the middle-aged or older audience to keep up their readership.

It becomes obvious, then, that our notions about old people and old age are changing. Getting old is no longer something to anticipate with fear. Life is not a straight line, the elderly are telling us. We no longer go from cradle to grave in a predictable way. With the right mental attitude, we can grow older than we ever thought possible and stay healthier and more alert longer. Along the way, we can experiment with many different lifestyles and jobs. We can retire, then return to work; we can live a fuller life than anyone in any previous century. Now it's society's turn to find ways of utilizing this older, healthier population in ways which will benefit both the young and the old.

Glossary

AGEISM. Prejudice against older people, like sexism or racism.

ALZHEIMER'S DISEASE. A mental disease similar to senility that commonly afflicts older people.

BABY BOOMERS. The generation of Americans born between 1946 and 1964.

CONVALESCENT HOSPITAL. A nursing home where elderly people are looked after and receive regular medical attention.

GERONTOLOGIST. A doctor who specializes in the process, effects and problems of aging.

HMO. Health Maintenance Organization. A group or association of doctors that provides medical care for members who pay regular dues.

MEDICARE, MEDICAID. Government programs designed to help the poor and elderly pay certain medical bills.

PARKINSON'S DISEASE. A nervous disorder recognizable by the uncontrollable trembling of a sufferer.

PREMIUM. The fee paid to an insurance company for protection against accident and illness.

SOCIAL SECURITY. The federal retirement program funded by payments from working Americans. After a person retires they receive a regular monthly payment from Social Security.

Bibliography

Boskey, James B., et al. *Teaching About Aging.*
University Press of America, 1982.

Curtin, Sharon. *Nobody Ever Died of Old Age.*
Boston: Atlantic Monthly Press, 1973.

Dychtwald, Ken and Joe Flower. *Age Wave.* Los
Angeles: Jeremy Tarcher, 1989.

Erikson, Erik H., ed. *Adulthood.* New York: W.W.
Norton, 1978.

Kendig, Hal L. *Ageing and Families.* London: Allen &
Unwin, 1986.

Levenson, Alvin and Dianna Porter. *An Introduction
to Gerontology and Geriatrics.* Springfield:
Charles C. Thomas Publishers, 1984.

McLeish, John A.B. *The Challenge of Aging.* Toronto:
Douglas & McIntyre, 1983.

INDEX

Photo Credits